Yves Ouellet

Photographs

Alain Dumas

TADOUSSAC

The Magnificent Bay

Translated by Alison Lee Strayer

Guy Saint-Jean
ÉDITEUR

Canadian Cataloguing in Publication Data

Ouellet, Yves, 1954-

Tadoussac: the magnificent bay

Translation of: Tadoussac: la baie des splendeurs.

Includes bibliographical references.

ISBN 2-89455-101-0

1. Tadoussac (Quebec) - Description and travel. 2. Tadoussac (Quebec) - History.
3. Tadoussac (Quebec) - Guidebooks. 4. Tadoussac (Quebec) - Pictorial works. I. Title.

FC2949.T3O9313 2000   971.4'17   C00-941022-8
F1054.5.T3O9313 2000

The publisher gratefully acknowledges the assistance of the Province
of Québec, through the SODEC (Société de développement des entreprises culturelles)
and the support of the Government of Canada,
through the Book Publishing Industry Development Program (BPIDP).

© Guy Saint-Jean Éditeur inc. 2000
© Photography Alain Dumas 2000
Translation: Alison Lee Strayer
Graphic Design: Zéro Faute, Outremont
Cover design: Bernard Langlois

Cover photography: Alain Dumas
and Pinsonneault & Frères, **Tadoussac**, s.d., ANQ-Q, P547, CPN 799-3
Legal Deposit second quarter 2000
Bibliothèque nationale du Québec and The National Library of Canada
ISBN 2-89455-101-0

The publisher would like to thank Mrs Gaby Villeneuve (Hôtel de ville de Tadoussac),
Mrs Edwige Munn (National Archives of Canada)
and Mrs Marcelle Cinq-Mars (historian) for iconographic research.

Guy Saint-Jean Éditeur inc.
3172, Boul. Industriel
Laval (Québec) Canada
H7L 4P7
Tel. (450) 663-1777
Fax (450) 663-6666
E-mail: saint-jean.editeur@qc.aira.com

Printed and bound in Canada

Table of Contents

Acknowledgements

Many thanks to:

The Government of Canada

Mr André Harvey, federal M.P. for Chicoutimi-Le Fjord

Saguenay–St. Lawrence Marine Park

Association touristique régionale de Manicouagan

Camping Tadoussac

Tourisme Québec

Croisières Famille Dufour

Mrs Gaby Villeneuve

Mr Benny Beattie

Maison du tourisme de la Côte-Nord

Aviation du Fjord inc.

Special thanks to:

Michel Boivin, codirector of the Saguenay–St. Lawrence Marine Park,

Marc Pagé (reviser), Jacques Hébert, Hugues Michaud, France Bernard, Natasha Savard, Gérard Thérien and the Marine Park team.

Municipality of Tadoussac: Pierre Marquis, Jacques Bussières, Monique Tremblay.

Patrice Poissant (Tourisme Québec), Christian Bouchard (ATR Manicouagan), Andrée Hardy (Maison du tourisme), the Boulianne family (Camping Tadoussac), Lisette Gagné (Musée maritime), Nancy Bolduc, Christelle Sartan, Mireille Héral (Maison des Dunes), Paulin Hovington and Lise Simard-Hovington (Gîte La Maison Hovington), Gérard Hugueney (Hôtel Georges), André Tremblay (Auberge de jeunesse de Tadoussac), Mr and Mrs Boutin (Domaine Bellevue), Alain Dufour (Croisières Famille Dufour), Marie-Thérèse Bournival, Michel Plourde, Nadine Cloutier, Manon Boucher (Centre Archéo-Topo des Bergeronnes), Serge Guimond (Station piscicole de Tadoussac), Rosaire McLean (Le Gibar), Bruno Therrien, Harold and Pam Price, Nicole Molson, Gita Beatty, Elizabeth O'Neil, Ann Dewart, Cheryl Turcot, Jessie Jamar and Charlotte Jamar, Evelyn Brooks and Sarah Brooks, the O'Neil, Dewart and Reilly families.

Many thanks to my close collaborators on this project: Joanne and Jennifer, Patrice Gauthier, Huguette Martin, Gilles Couturier, Alfred Martin and Jocelyne, André Côté and Yolaine, les Randonneurs du Saguenay.

"The boat just docked at Tadoussac, a little nest of greenery tucked into the mountainside, and near-famous for its ancient-ness.

Huge rocks loom up, haughty and proud, indescribably majestic and disdainful of the weak and tiny mortals who walk at their feet below.

Truly this is virgin nature at her greatest, untamed, unconquered and always grandiose. The sight is both terrible and sublime; it fascinates, subjugates us like those infinite mysteries of which the eye can never get its fill.

In some places, however, the mountainsides are covered with rich and luxuriant vegetation. The startling green of fir trees, larches, the flashing white of birches lend yet another kind of charm to this picturesque landscape and seem to animate its haughty and pretentious physiognomy, as if with a smile..."

ROBERTINE BARRY, 1895

My Tadoussac

spell and since that time, my state of enchantment has never changed or faded. In fact, the more I've gotten to know Tadoussac, its key role in the history of Quebec and the New World, the infinite complexity and diversity of its marine life, the fabulous world of whales, the outsized landscape of the Saguenay fjord as well as the very specific culture shared by the people of Tadoussac, the more I knew this delightful village was going to have a profound effect on many aspects of my life.

But we do not really have to know all this in order to appreciate Tadoussac and its charms. The simple fact of being here makes me feel transformed, and judging from the radiant look of the crowds strolling around Tadoussac, there is no doubt in my mind that others feel the same. It has to do with the wide open spaces, the vast panoramic view combined with the intimacy of the little village. Perhaps it is Tadoussac's long history as a holiday spot that helps create this atmosphere of leisure and wonder combined. For me it is the emotional charge, the feeling of adventure and freedom that Tadoussac inspires, that makes me so profoundly attached to the

Nowhere else in Quebec, and in only a few places in North America, can sites as extraordinary as Tadoussac be found. With its magical atmosphere, rich history and incredibly luxuriant environment, Tadoussac is decidedly unique.

From the very first time I set foot in Tadoussac, it exerted its full powers of seduction upon me. I literally fell under its

place. It is the whales and the remarkable bodies of water that collide in the Saguenay River estuary, unforgettable evenings on the dunes watching the sun explode against Ile Rouge before sinking below the horizon. Then there's the South Shore lighting up, winking and shimmering until nightfall, the lights from lighthouses and buoys that begin their synchronous choreography, criss-crossed by the slow and indifferent sweep of ship lights beneath an immense sky pierced with tiny flashes of brilliance.

I love Tadoussac for all the things about it that cannot be put into words, for the shiver that goes down my spine each time I see the plunging cleavage of Anse-à-l'Eau and the boats that dare venture into the turbulent waters washing up around the stone nipples. At such moments, life changes pace; all at once, it grows lighter. The mind grows wide as the horizon, and the horizon overflows into infinity. At such times, I feel as if I'm diving back into the past to meet Cartier, Champlain, Chauvin, Anadabijou, Labrosse, the Prices, Coverdale, Molson, Beattie, the boat-builders, the lightkeepers, the boat pilots, the Hovingtons, Bouliannes, and Brissons, the Côtés, Tremblays, Villeneuves and all the others whose names have been etched in history, great and small.

The St. Lawrence carries my dreams on long boats that file out to sea towards faraway shores. I never tire of breathing the wind of the dunes, of trying to touch the fog, seize the clouds creeping over the sand, or guess where the little whale will

Visitors come by the thousands to meet the whales off Tadoussac.

emerge after feasting in the seabed near shore. Only in Tadoussac have I known so many states of grace, for it is sea and fjord, bay and islands, coast and horizon all at once. So many marvels does it share, and so generously, with the travelers who come from far and wide having heard it is a place with many unusual things to see, do, savour and experience.

I also love Tadoussac for its changing character, very peaceful in winter, calm in the spring, bustling with activity in summer

page 11

A large freighter at the mouth of the Saguenay fjord.

Even in winter, the beauty of the landscape is breathtaking.

Autumn in Tadoussac with its ochres and yellows.

Morning fog invades the bay.

and spectacular in the fall. I love it for its obstinately unstable climate — and Tadoussac weather can go from stormy to heavenly, hot to cold, fog to clearing, dark cloud to azure sky, angry winds to dead calm, over a day or even just a few hours.

No less varied are the sights and sounds of the changing tides that rise and

Ferries passing each other between Anse-à-l'Eau and Baie-Sainte-Catherine.

fall in the bay, alternately covering and baring the beach and rocks. Tadoussac also transforms according to the angle from which one views it. Depending on whether one sees it from the waterfront promenade or the heights of the fjord, the campground, the sea, the lookout by the cross, the dunes to the north of Highway 138, Pointe Rouge, Pointe-de-l'Islet or from the village, Tadoussac is remarkably changeable. Our natural reference points are the Hôtel's scarlet roof, the village

trademark, or the magnificent fjord, its most striking feature.

The sounds of Tadoussac are another dimension of its unique character. First there is the lament, almost a concert, of the foghorns that resonate as the first traces of mist form over the icy waters. Early-bird tourists taking a jog on the beach sometimes mistake the sound for whalesong. I am at once soothed and transfixed by the foghorns' long plaintive moan.

But Tadoussac's truly original sound is the ferry boats' departure signal that echoes back and forth, day and night, between Anse-à-l'Eau and Anse-du-Portage. Each time a ferry pulls away from the wharf, the echo can be heard over the entire territory of Tadoussac, from Moulin-Baude to Pointe-de-l'Islet. The sound leaves no doubt as to where we are, for only in Tadoussac does the ferry-call resonate in this way.

The tapestry of sound is further coloured by the cry of the gulls, the breaking of the waves, the roar of boat motors and the voices of visitors conversing in different languages, transforming this little summer community into the most cosmopolitan village in Quebec.

The most fascinating aspect of Tadoussac is the historic dimension. It would be unthinkable to visit Tadoussac without taking an interest in its history.

Largely due to its strategic location, it became the site of an incomparable epic, which is why it can now call itself the "first permanent European settlement north of

Mexico": older than Quebec City, founded in 1608, older than Plymouth where the Pilgrims settled in 1620. In 1600 the Huguenot Pierre de Chauvin de Tonnetuit, captain of King Henri IV's merchant marine, founded the first trading post in the New World and thus laid the foundations for the oldest village on the continent, officially launching the economic activity that would give birth to New France: the fur trade. Tadoussac would come to play a key role as a port, especially because it was the only port on the St. Lawrence for thirty years. Of course, the history of Tadoussac and its inhabitants has had its high points and its low points. Periods of great activity were followed by periods of inactivity, but Tadoussac has survived thanks to the fur trade, forestry, tourism, marine mammal observation cruises, and other secondary activities. After all this time, as we head into the new millenium, Tadoussac may enjoy its status as the first North American village to have existed over four centuries of history.

It is my hope that by reading this book, you too will come to know and appreciate this charming and picturesque little hamlet.

Tadoussac Bay.

Impressions

Looking down from the big dunes that surround Tadoussac Bay like a gigantic natural amphitheatre, we cannot help but succumb to the charm of this magnificent circular bay. It seems dwarfed by those titans, the St. Lawrence, the Saguenay fjord and the mountains of the Canadian Shield. Bordered by a fine fringe of blonde sand and a wide strand generously bared by the retreating tide, we can see laughing children playing in the little salt water pools. A few vacationers pull their chairs forward as the bank recedes. Young swimmers brave the icy water that swells up from the sea bed. A group of kayakers barely ruffle the water's surface as they pass, while little whales frolic merrily in the waves. Earlier a herd of belugas swam past, heading for the Saguenay. The bay comes alive when boats of all sizes return from whale-watching, then leave again filled with hundreds of bedazzled daytrippers who will soon have stories to tell about their encounters with some of the biggest living creatures on earth. As all this activity unfolds, leisurely walkers look on, strolling along the boardwalk that curves around the bay, just like the first vacationers to visit the area 150 years ago. A blaze of scarlet in the heart of the village marks the Grand Hôtel, a common reference point.

Tadoussac Bay has always been a meeting place. It was here that the Natives assembled every summer, long before the arrival of the white man.

It was here that Whites and Natives came together in 1603 to found a new world, here that vacationers from all over the continent have arrived in droves for a century. It is here that the great marine mammals gather after their voyage around the globe,

here that incredible bodies of water meet head on. Globetrotters come to this very special part of Quebec in search of the most singular sights, and some of the richest and strongest, most authentic and spectacular experiences on earth.

Let us not forget that this is also the home of a population who has every reason to be proud of its roots, ancestors

and milieu: men and women, scarcely a thousand of them, some of whose families have been in the region for a very long time whereas others are more recent settlers. The tourist industry, national parks, scientific research, the arts, commerce and services ensure their survival in this enclave of stone and sand that has sometimes proved thankless for those who attempt to stick it out year round, live there, watch their children grow up there. They have always been open to the world and shared their summer paradise, to find themselves together again come winter, in a seaside village that is unique among the hamlets of the North Shore.

This bay, which has been officially deemed one of the most beautiful in the world, can only be described in superlatives.

In spite of the development of tourism in Tadoussac Bay, it has retained its natural untamed character and its face of a bucolic little coastal village nestled in a monumental natural arena. Here, the passage of time and history is as tangible as the salt air and seaspray. Tadous-

sac's horizons never cease to amaze with their nuances and contrasts between morning and night, sun and cloud, summer and winter, cold and balmy weather. Here we can commune with the majesty and mystery of the elements, and establish a vital contact with the forces and beauties of nature. Tadoussac Bay plunges us back into ourselves, our profound nature and its potential for happiness.

The bay is unique in North America, and this we can affirm beyond the shadow of a doubt. Today it falls under the auspices of two national parks and numerous organizations that see to its preservation. Its membership in the World's Most Beautiful Bays Club further ensures the conservation of its precious natural and cultural heritage.

A pivotal point

Located in an extraordinary setting of mountains and water, rock face and greenery 222 kilometres northeast of Quebec City, the village stands at the border of the North Shore region and Saguenay Fjord mouth. It also borders on the Charlevoix and Saguenay regions, which makes it a true pivotal point in terms of both geography and tourism. It is an open door on the immense untamed territories of northern and northwestern Quebec, a strategic and easily-accessed location, three hours from Quebec City.

"**It is a place full of mountains so high**, one might imagine that the giants of yore who wanted to fight the sky threw down stones in this place to make their ascent.
Among these rocks the great St. Lawrence River makes a bay or cove that serves as a port for ships that sail in these lands: we call this bay Tadoussac.
Nature made it commodious for the anchoring of vessels, having built it round and sheltered from the winds."

The Jesuit Relations

The village of Tadoussac is made up of four distinct historical and geographical sectors:

1. The Shore
2 The Village
3. L'Anse-à-l'Eau
4. Moulin-Baude

Jonction 172 et 138 à 4 km
Crossroad 172 and 138 at 4 km

des Érables
des Ormes
des Bouleaux
des Peupliers
des Bois-Francs
des Chênes

Route 138

de la Montagne
Bellevue
des Forgerons Nord

Père Labrosse
Pont-Gravé

4.

Secteur du
Moulin à Baude
(Maison des Dunes)
*Moulin à Baude Area
(The Dunes House)*

Dunes de Sable

Pointe Rouge

du Bateau Passeur

2.

Hôtel-de-Ville
Jacques-Cartier
Chauvin
des Montagnais

des Pionniers
des Jésuites
Morin

des Pionniers

Lac l'Anse l'Eau lake

du Bateau Passeur

vers Moulin à Baude
to Moulin à Baude

Sentier de la plage
vers la Maison des Dunes
Seaside trail to the Dunes House

Traversier Ferry to vers Québec Québec

«Sentier de la Coupe»

du Parc
Coupe de l'Islet
des Bateliers
Saguenay

Grand Hôtel

Bord de l'Eau

Bord de l'Eau

Baie de Tadoussac
Tadoussac Bay

1.

de la Cale Sèche

3.

Quai
Wharf

«Sentier de la Pointe»

Pointe de l'Islet

Different periods...

Above, circa 1864; centre, 1942; below, circa 1867.

Next page: centre, circa 1945; above, 1999 and circa 1868; below, 1871 and 1999.

As early as the 19th Century, Tadoussac Bay welcomed merchant vessels and, of course, tourists.

TADOUSSAC

The waters
of Tadoussac Bay

A bay on two estuaries

THANKS TO ITS UNIQUE LOCATION on two estuaries, Tadoussac Bay is fed by two sources at once: from the St. Lawrence estuary and waters from the Saguenay fjord, straight ahead of the bay.

Tadoussac Bay is actually part of the Saguenay fjord estuary, which continues up to four kilometres off the St. Lawrence estuary and affects an area that extends far beyond Tadoussac Bay.

The land gradually rose again, freeing the territory of what was called the Champlain Sea. Charlevoix, Tadoussac's neighbour, is one of the most earthquake-prone zones in North America. This may be due to isostatic re-elevation, the converging of chunks of the earth's crust in front of the Charlevoix region or the weakness of the Logan fault. However, we cannot say for sure.

Sculpted by glaciers

Glaciers had an important role to play in creating the relief of the Laurentians as we know them today. This part of the continent was subject to several glacial advances, the most recent of which was 12,000 years ago. Masses of ice, three to five kilometres thick, greatly eroded the mountain cover that lay along their path, scattering moraine, sand, clay, gravel and various debris on their retreat.

The phenomenal weight of the glaciers literally crushed the land down to a level which, in the Tadoussac region, was 180 metres deeper than the present level.

Navigation presents many dangers...

The Great Lakes route

Tadoussac would not exist without the St. Lawrence River. This giant shaped the North Shore littoral split, but more than that, it shaped the life of its inhabitants according to the shifting of tides, fishing, currents and seasons of the sea.

The region is located at the beginning of the St. Lawrence estuary, that is, between the middle estuary and the Gulf of St. Lawrence. Running north/northeast, the estuary is at the border of the two main geological regions of Quebec, the Canadian Shield to the north and the Appalachians to the south.

Tadoussac Bay is located at the southern limit of the Canadian Shield and the Laurentians mountain range, which is made up of some of the oldest rocks in the world. Most of them are four billion years old, which takes us back to the Pre-Cambrian era.

Still, the St. Lawrence between Baie-Saint-Paul and Tadoussac is relatively shallow, ten to sixty metres deep on average. The tides, which become stronger the further we move up the estuary, are between four and six metres high.

Commercial navigation greatly depends on two channels. The one most used is the north channel, two to three kilometres

> "**The river's** many hazards and its navigation, which is as dangerous and difficult as can be, are the best possible ramparts for the city of Quebec."
>
> **Louis-Antoine de Bougainville, 1756**

Le Haut-fond Prince (Prince shallows)

Major shallows can be observed around Tadoussac Bay, including the Haut-fond Prince (Prince shallows), on which the Prince of Wales ran aground on August 18, 1860 with his ship the HMS **Hero**, in foggy weather.

The shallows were created by a glacial constriction that formed at the mouth of the Saguenay fjord, whose moraine deposits extend four kilometres out to sea from Tadoussac Bay.

After that, the Prince shallows shared their name with a lightship that sat at anchor to warn passing vessels. The **Haut-Fond-Prince #7**, like a similar boat stationed at the Saguenay River mouth, was stripped of its motor and equipped with powerful signal lights. By day it was easily identifiable by the name painted in big white letters on its red and black hull.

The lightships of the St. Lawrence were used from about 1830 to 1960. The sailors endured the sea's movements day after day and week after week, working in harsh conditions that gravely compromised their health and safety.

wide and ten to seventy metres deep. It is thanks to this channel that we can see so many big boats off the coast, heading for the Great Lakes. These freighters or container transporters are obliged to follow this route.

Difficult navigation

The waters off Tadoussac are considered some of the most hazardous in the entire St. Lawrence, with violent currents, shallows, tides, reefs, fogs and various climatic phenomena, on top of intense river traffic. Indeed, 2,000 merchant vessels travel the river each year, as well as cruise boats and pleasure craft.

"La Toupie"

Retired in 1955, the lightship **Haut-Fond-Prince** was replaced (but only nine years later) by a steel structure built on the sea bed, soon nicknamed "la Toupie" (the spinning top). It consisted of a xenon lantern which on a clear night produced 300,000 candlepower units of light, increased to 32,000,000 units when fog moved in. In foggy weather, deep sounds were emitted by three diaphones at intervals of three to fifteen seconds.

Life conditions on the cramped lightpillars were just as arduous as on the lightships. Lightkeepers could not bring their families and had to live without privacy, and in constant fear of storms.

On December 25, 1966, a distress message was sent when the pillar, designed to resist waves of eight metres, was struck by waves of fourteen metres high.

"There's a terrible storm at the Pilier. A chassis has been smashed by waves. Water's pouring in like a river by the door of the 51. The floors are flooded. The heating has quit. The pipes have been ripped out. Call Quebec. The Pilier is shaking so badly, it's frightening. Our lives are in danger. If we have to bail..."

The lighthouses of Ile Rouge and the Prince shallows were the last two St. Lawrence stations to be automated, in 1988.

Lights of
Tadoussac

A magical night on the bay.

AT NIGHTFALL the towns and villages on the South Shore across from Tadoussac light up in a slow crescendo. Then Rivière-du-Loup, upstream, lights up after the violence of sunset, and Trois-Pistoles, downstream, emerges from shadow. Between the two is a long parenthesis of darkness, made darker by Ile Verte (Notre-Dame-des-Sept-Douleurs) at the mouth of the fjord, which hides the lights of the Lower St. Lawrence for eleven kilometres. In the middle of this black curtain an explosion of light sends out regular flashes. Built in 1809, the Ile Verte lighthouse was the first on the St. Lawrence and remained the only one until 1830.

The dunes offer the best view of the criss-crossing beams from the lighthouse, beacons, and buoys, flashing with invariable regularity like a strange ghostly dance.

From some places on the dunes one can see the lighthouse beams from the Haut-fond Prince, Ile Rouge and Ile Verte in harmonious alignment. On either side of this sparkling trail of light, other navigational beams can be observed: from Ile Bicquette downstream, near Rimouski, from Ile Long-Pèlerin upstream, or the beacons of Pointe-Noire across the Saguenay.

Add to these sporadic glimmers the green and red lights of marking buoys along the St. Lawrence channel and the Saguenay access channel, outlining the route used by pleasure craft as well as some of the biggest ships in the world.

The pilots

For centuries, ships have called upon specially trained pilots to assist them in navigating the difficult waters of the St. Lawrence estuary between Tadoussac and Quebec City. As early as 1635, the Collège des Jésuites de Québec started training St. Lawrence river pilots, who at that time got on board at Moulin-Baude, one league from Tadoussac.

Under the English Régime, from 1762, the role of the pilots became official, but this did not prevent sixty boats from going down between 1776 and 1783.

The Pilot's house on the pointe de l'Islet.

The *Marie-Clarisse* at the mouth of the Saguenay.

Today, all the big ships that pass off Tadoussac have a pilot on board from the station at Les Escoumins.

The Saguenay River is no less feared by navigators who, in the nineteenth century, used pilots to sail their schooners up to Chicoutimi. The most famous of them, Eugène Boulanger, would go meet ships at Ile Rouge to take them to Saguenay. Around 1880 he built "la maison du pilote", the pilot's house, a charming blue dwelling near the Centre d'interprétation des mammifères marins (CIMM) that has been owned by the Price family since 1920.

Ile Rouge

I've had my eye on it for years, watched it grow dark in the red-glowing dusk in prelude to the most limpid of sunsets, to emerge again with the first rays of dawn. I had heard about it on marine radio. Fisheries and Oceans Canada weather forecasts refer to the station on the island and report weather conditions in the middle of the river, the middle of nowhere. There are days when the wind pushes the fog along the St. Lawrence until it lifts like a thick curtain to reveal the river. Suddenly the little island appears with startling clarity, magnified by the mist and coloured bright scarlet by the sun's ardour, a phenomenon surely noticed by Samuel de

Champlain, who named it in 1626. From the heights of Tadoussac it is easy to identify, located right in the middle of the estuary, thirteen kilometres out from the mouth of the Saguenay and about the same distance from the coast of Notre-Dame-des-Sept-Douleurs in the Lower St. Lawrence. One can distinguish its squat lighthouse, dating from 1848. We can even see each of the little red and white buildings dotting the pebble beach, 600 metres long and 150 metres wide.

Profile of the Fjord

THE SAGUENAY RIVER contains the fourth largest basin in Quebec and is the most important tributary of the St. Lawrence, next to the Outaouais River. The estuary receives 90% of the overflow from Lac Saint-Jean, whose circumference is 225 kilometres and whose surface area is 1,048.9 km². Its basin covers 78,000 km² and its average speed is 1,300 m²/s. It is divided into three parts, including the river as such, from Lac Saint-Jean to the outskirts of Chicoutimi, a distance of about 95 kilometres. The pre-fjord starts a few kilometres from Chicoutimi (Shipshaw) and stretches to the Saint-Fulgence littoral split, where the fjord itself is some 100 kilometres long.

Tadoussac Bay is located at the mouth of the Saguenay fjord, separated from it by only a rock ridge.

Special features

The existence of a fjord depends on several factors, such as a valley forged by the passage of one or several glaciers, U-shaped with steep and forbidding rock sides.

Fjords like the Saguenay are linked to the sea at one end and receive an influx of fresh water at the other, creating a mixture of fresh and salt water.

The Saguenay also has a rock sill at its mouth or a transverse glacial constriction formed by more resistant rock masses and moraine residues pushed by the glacier. The rock sill of the Saguenay extends up to four kilometres beyond the river mouth and is preceded by a 275 metre trench a short distance upstream from Tadoussac.

Fjords in general can be recognized by a very pronounced layering of waters. Close to the surface, as the water deepens, there is a rapid change in salinity, temperature and density that creates a layer called "thermo-halocline". This is the result of fresh and relatively warm tributary water flowing over the mass of cold salt water below. These cold salty waters, which come from the St. Lawrence estuary and Gulf, flow over the glacial constriction into the depths of the fjord.

In July, surface waters attain temperatures from 18 °C and 20 °C. This surface layer is ten to fifteen metres thick. The thermo-halocline layer is an intermediary layer, about thirteen meters thick on average, where the temperature drops to about 1 °C. Beneath this layer, at a depth of about twenty metres, is the deep layer that extends down to the fjord bed, where temperatures fluctuate between 0,4 and 1,7 °C, and where the water is extraordinarily clear.

The mass of sea water that flows into the Saguenay by the river mouth circulates

in an upstream direction, that is, in the opposite direction from the flow of fresh water at the surface. Less dense and less heavy, the fresh water from Lac Saint-Jean and the Saguenay tributaries literally slides over top of the salt water flowing towards the St. Lawrence.

The Saguenay Fjord is about a hundred kilometres long and varies from two to four kilometres wide, which makes it one of the biggest fjords in the world. It occupies a deep gash in the Laurentians, hemmed in by steep cliffs that are 150 metres tall on average, in some places as tall as 400 metres, as at Cap Trinité (411 m) and Cap Éternité (457 m).

Between Sainte-Rose-du-Nord and Anse-Saint-Jean, the fjord attains a depth of up to 276 metres, about 170 metres more than the bed of the St. Lawrence on either side of Ile Rouge. In front of Ile Saint-Louis, the bottom plunges down to a depth of 180 metres, then up again in front of Baie Sainte-Marguerite, then back down to 250 metres before reaching the river mouth.

However, the results of recent studies reveal surprising data about the real depth of the fjord. According to this data, the accumulation of sediment on the Saguenay river bottom is as much as 1,400 metres thick in some places, almost five times the maximum depth of the Saguenay today. This means the real depth of the Saguenay Fjord is over 2,000 metres, if we take account of the present relief above sea level.

The meeting of the waters.

The meeting
of the waters

Tadoussac Bay is right in the middle of the zone affected by the Saguenay fjord, where fresh water from the river meets salt water from the St. Lawrence, colliding without dissolving and provoking impressive movements that can be readily seen. Straight out from the shores of Tadoussac, the currents clash like Titans, causing turbulence at the surface and preventing the water from freezing in winter.

This turbulent border where waters meet is called "panache". By inflatable boat, it is obvious when one is passing over it due to the waves and the clearly visible white line in the water.

Some of the strongest currents in the St. Lawrence are found at Tadoussac, because of the radical reduction in the depth of the sea bed in front of Tadoussac Bay, and the narrowing of the river mouth. These impetuous waters that flow by the bay can reach speeds of up to seven knots at high tide. They reach maximum speeds of 3,000 m³/ second as compared to the average yearly speed of 1,300 m³/ second.

Traces
of the past

ence on the North Shore about 8,000 years ago, a revelation of great importance. The Centre Archéo-Topo de Grandes-Bergeronnes highlights this phase of prehistory.

The archaic era

Numerous elements also give us information about the archaic era, 8,000 to 4,000 B.C., and the forestry era, 1,000 B.C. to the arrival of Jacques Cartier.

Humans that inhabited the Tadoussac region during the archaic era were already living off the sea. Archaeological sites abound in bone fragments from beavers, seals and belugas, and to a lesser degree, fish and shore birds. Rigorous analyses of objects discovered (bones, knives, scrapers, adzes) suggest that the sea was a vital resource for those inhabitants of Tadoussac Bay and the surrounding area.

Prehistory

There are important archaeological sites at the confluence of the Saguenay and the St. Lawrence estuary, and digs in the Tadoussac sector play an important role in uncovering the history of the North American continent. These sites have much to tell us about the routes taken by the most ancient inhabitants of the region and where they settled. The territory of Quebec has probably been inhabited for 11,000 years on the South Shore of the St. Lawrence. The Tadoussac region, especially the Cap-de-Bon-Désir sector, is turning up more and more vestiges of the "paleo-Indian" period. Evidence discovered in 1999 by the team of archaeologist Michel Plourde at Cap-de-Bon-Désir points to a First Nations pres-

The forestry era

Archaeologists are more familiar with the more recent forestry (or silvicultural) era. Pottery fragments from the middle and late forestry era can be linked to two traditions, the most signficant of which is the Algonquin. Numerous objects of Iroquois origin lead us to understand that St. Lawrence Iroquois of the Quebec City region also frequented Tadoussac, which has been a meeting place for ancient civilizations since several centuries before the arrival of Jacques Cartier. It is more than likely that Tadoussac has been a hunting and fishing paradise for a very long time.

The grottoes

Up among the cliffs over the Saguenay River mouth, only a few kilometres from Tadoussac, are three grottoes that were discovered and explored in the late 1940s. They eloquently confirm the presence of First Nations peoples in the bay area. Some thousand artefacts have been found in the grottoes, identified with the three main Montagnais groups in the region: the Papinachois of Tadoussac, the Chicoutimiens of the shores of the Saguenay, and the Kakouchacs of Lac Saint-Jean.

Totouskak

In prehistoric times, Tadoussac was already well known and frequented, which gives rise to several theories about where it got its name. The most common explanation is that the Montagnais (some say it was Algonquins) called it **Tatouskak**, plural of **totouswk** or **totochak**, meaning "breasts": an allusion to the two round sandy hills on the west side of the village. The Montagnais also said **Uashaushtekuek**, meaning "where the river mouth is".

Ethnologist and ethnolinguist José Mailhot holds that **Tadoussac** comes from the Micmac word **Gtatosag** meaning "between the rocks". This name would have been used by French sailors in the Gulf of St. Lawrence in the sixteenth century. The name appears in European documents as of 1586. Even though the Micmacs lived on the South Shore of the St. Lawrence, they regularly travelled to the mouth of the Saguenay, so it is not surprising that their language has a word for this place.

Moreover, we have come across different spellings of Tadoussac, one of the oldest place names in the New World. Spellings include **Tadousac** (seventeenth and eighteenth centuries), **Tadoussak**, **Thadoyzeau** (1550). The word **Tadosa** appears on the map called **Creuxius Tabula Novæ Français** (1660), **Tadouscu** on the map of Hakluyt-Wright (1599-1600) and **Tadoucaq** on that of Guillaume Levasseur (1601). Père Labrosse (1758) wrote it in Latin, **Tadussaki** and **Tadussakum**, and Samuel de Champlain (1603) wrote **Tadoufac**, the "s" in those times being written as "f".

The first Europeans

Braving the many dangers of the sea, the first Europeans to approach Tadoussac were Norman and Breton fishermen and whalehunters who came to the banks of Newfoundland around the end of the sixteenth century. They landed on the coast just long enough to transform the products of their labours before taking them back to Europe.

Though it is difficult to confirm that the Basques entered the Tadoussac sector before 1545, geographer André Thévet reported in **Le grand insulaire** that "tall pilots, having navigated several dangerous spots, probably the North Shore, arrived at the river and Saguenay country. The region is the best for fishing because a great number of whales still frolic there and are much in demand by the Bayonnais and Spanish".

Jacques Cartier came in 1535, during his second voyage, and noted that the Iroquois hunted sea elephant. We can also affirm that from 1580, the fur trade was flourishing.

Adze

European axe

Trumpet Pipe, clay and sand

Gouge, 4,000 years, used in woodworking

Arrowheads

Seal bones, tympanum and canine

Potteries from the Quebec City region, brought to the North Shore by sealhunters

A Kingdom

Tadoussac is at the heart of what has been called for almost five centuries the "Kingdom of Saguenay". Jacques Cartier himself first referred to it this way in his Relation of 1535-1536. Two Iroquois from Stadaconé whom he brought back from France on his second voyage introduced the country, which he was admiring from the sea, as "a kingdom called Saguenay, where people dress as they do in France and where there are mines of red copper".

To this day, the expression "Kingdom of Saguenay" has been used by explorers and authors alike. It has been adopted by popular and local tradition, and is still common usage.

Birthplace of New France

Tadoussac both fascinated and terrified the first white men to approach its granite cliffs, unpredictable currents and austere shores. Though this tiny speck on the map was considered the capital of the New World fur trade, its climate and extreme relief would have gotten the better of Europeans without help from the local masters, the Montagnais.

Towards the end of the sixteenth century, the French government became increasingly interested in what Voltaire would later call "a few acres of snow". So as to "promote" (as it claimed) colonization and exploit valuable resources, it appealed to the royal Court to obtain the monopoly for the developing fur trade in New France.

In 1599, Pierre de Chauvin acquired this right and in exchange, promised to settle fifty colonists per year in the area (for a total of 500).

With the aim of improving business he chose Tadoussac, due to the collaboration with the Montagnais, the quality of Saguenay furs and the availability of provisions.

In 1600, Chauvin built a trading post. To fulfil his promise to colonize New France, he lodged sixteen men for one winter in a fortified house. Only five survived, with the help of the Montagnais. The Chauvin house, inhabited from that period on, was operated by the Hudson's Bay Company until 1852 then rebuilt in 1942 by William-

"It was a country cottage, four toises long and three toises wide, eight feet tall, covered with boards, with a fireplace in the middle; a house in the shape of a guardroom, surrounded by rocks and a small ditch filled with sand. A little stream ran below."

Samuel de Champlain, 1603

Hugh Coverdale. It was the first permanent dwelling in New France and all of North America.

Samuel de Champlain, founder of Quebec City and father of New France, left us a description of the place after his sojourn of 1603.

The reconstructed Maison Chauvin still stands today in the middle of the village, in almost the same spot as the original, with the same little stream beside it.

The alliance

On May 27 and 28, 1603, Pointe-aux-Alouettes, on Baie Sainte-Catherine, was the setting for another important event in the history of New France: the finalizing of the first pact between the French and the native Indians. A large number of Montagnais, with their Algonquian and Etchemin allies, celebrated their victory over their common enemy, the Iroquois. Anchoring their ships in Tadoussac harbour, Champlain and Pontgravé returned from France with two Natives who told their compatriots and their chief, Anadabijou, about all they had seen on the other side of the "big lake". Their account was so convincing and so full of praise that Champlain and the great Sagamo, in a tobacco ceremony, sealed an important pact whereby the French were allowed to colonize the country in exchange for providing military support against the Iroquois.

This agreement would last for over 150 years, until the English conquest. Its consequences can still be felt in Quebec society today.

The passage

Very soon, long before the trading posts at Quebec and Trois-Rivières, the Tadoussac post became the "infallible passage". Thanks to the Montagnais, ships were met

with canoes full of furs from the Saguenay, which served as a channel to an inland sea fed by powerful tributaries that stocked a continent-wide fur pool.

The fur route

The fur route used by the Montagnais runs up the Saguenay for 130 kilometres, requiring a journey of two to three days, paddling from morning to night. At the rapids, which are unnavigable, the route continues by land along the Chicoutimi River, requiring seven portages over eight kilometres — in other words, one long day. After Lake Kenogami, the route continues without obstacles for some distance, then reaches a series of short portages leading to Belle Rivière, a way of entry into Lac Saint-Jean.

Another day's travel, then another along the south shore of the lake to the Ashuapmushuan river, the least difficult route to the great Lac Mistassini. Just before Mistassini, the waters of the Chigoubiche river and Lac Nicabau merge at 400 metres above sea level. From this point on, there is easy access to Lac Mistassini then James Bay.

Incredible though it may seem, the Montagnais took only about twenty days to get from Tadoussac to James Bay.

Fall of the fur trade

In the years that followed, the fur trade was the main human and economic activity in Tadoussac. The port was described as feverishly busy, and became even more so with the founding of Quebec City in 1608, when Tadoussac became the landing point for goods and persons arriving from France as well as the boarding point for passengers and goods traveling across the ocean. However, from the mid seventeenth century on, economic activity stimulated by the fur trade gradually moved towards Quebec and Trois-Rivières, which finally upstaged Tadoussac until the English conquest.

The Indian Chapel

The Indian Chapel

In 1615, some Récollet priests attempted to establish a first mission at Tadoussac, but the Natives, being nomadic, just passed through. This endeavour, like that of the Jesuits in 1632, was bound to fail. However, Father Jean Dequen, discoverer of Lac Saint-Jean, met with more success in 1641.

In 1747, Tadoussac once again distinguished itself in the historic landscape of New France. Father Coquart erected a magnificent little chapel devoted to Saint Anne that would become one of the preferred places of worship for the North Shore Montagnais. This chapel still stands facing Tadoussac Bay and is the oldest wooden chapel on the North American continent. Its 250th anniversary was celebrated with great pomp in 1997. Its cemetery movingly evokes the human history of Tadoussac, and still contains the remains of Jesuits who played such an important role in that history, Father Coquart and Father de la Brosse.

The very first chapel in Tadoussac, probably made of stone, was destroyed in the fire of 1645. Its bell, brought from France, still hangs in the present wood chapel.

"**My first sketch** shows the little old chapel, said to be the first of its kind to be erected by the French in America. It is a wooden building. Inside, it measures 25 by 30 feet, and contains a very elegant altar and other fixtures in an octogonal alcove at the very back.
The altar painting shows the crucifixion.
To the left are two other paintings: one a portrait of the first priest to arrive in Canada, the other a biblical scene.
To the right is a picture of an angel guiding a small child. The rounded ceiling is painted blue.
At the other end of the chapel from the altar is a little balcony, and on the floor, rough planks for the faithful."

Lossing-Barrit, 1859

Moulin-Baude

LOCATED at the eastern end of Tadoussac, Moulin-Baude was once a separate entity, more a hamlet than a village. It was called Mol Baudet, Moulin Baudet, mollin Baudé, Molin Bode, Molinbault and Moulin à Baude. The name most often used today is Moulin-Baude. The name was in use from the late sixteenth century, long before any mill existed in the sector, and at a period when the site was physically quite different from what it is now. According to historian Danny Desbiens, "the left bank of the river of Moulin-Baude used to end in a point that jutted out into the St. Lawrence, forming a natural bay." This point ended in two isolated capes that sailors called "Old Man Baude and his Missus". Desbiens explains that "the name of the mill came from a corruption of the word 'mole' (jetty), meaning a structure built to protect the entrance to a port". This hypothesis was confirmed by the Lescarbot map (1609), which identified the place as "Mol Baudet". Champlain, in 1603, considered the sector a natural extension of the Tadoussac harbour and an excellent place to drop anchor. It was in the protected bay of Moulin-Baude that ships of 300 tons or more cast anchor at the end of their Atlantic crossing. Thus according to

Desbiens, Moulin-Baude could be considered the first deep-water port in North America.

Today's navigators find this hard to believe, especially kayakers who at low tide cannot even find enough water for a kayak on the sandbar at Pointe-aux-Vaches. Indeed, an extraordinary event radically transformed this part of the shore: the earthquake of 1663. On Tuesday, February 5 at 5:30 a.m., the "wrath of God" hit, and a terrible tremour carried off the cape that Champlain had named "Pointe de tous les Diables". Landslides filled the harbour and the port of Moulin-Baude disappeared forever.

"Some mountains that have been engulfed can no longer be seen," reports the **Jesuit Relations** of 1663.

The same upheaval was observed at Les Éboulements, Charlevoix after the earthquake.

The forming
of the "Dunes"

Another natural phenomenon that would forever change the destiny of the Moulin-Baude sector was the formation of sandbanks. They are called "the dunes" but they are actually marine plateaus that took about 10,000 years to form after the glaciers started to retreat in the northwest part of the continent. The territory was then submerged by the Goldthwait Sea, leaving significant clay and sand deposits behind. Once freed of the ice, several kilometres thick, the earth's crust gradually rose again, forming the two marine plateaus of the Dunes. With the centuries, enough humus and vegetation grew that the soil became arable by 1838, about the same time as the village's first economic boom. Moulin-

Baude was Tadoussac's garden until the beginning of the twentieth century, when a period of desertification and silting left the earth barren. Only one farm survived the onslaught of the dunes, which nature seems to be gradually taming: a few decades ago, the landsape was even more desert-like than now. In 1845, Thomas Simard founded a sawmill that would lead to the founding of the hamlet. For the next 120 years, Moulin-Baude had three saw-mills, one flour mill, and a hydroelectric station at the foot of the waterfall near the beach, in operation from 1938 to 1965. The intensity of the electrical current varied according to the river speed.

Hovington farm,
the last in Moulin-Baude.

The lime kilns

"This entire country is marble" wrote Father Charlevoix after passing through Moulin-Baude in 1726. What he was in fact referring to was lime carbonate of great purity that was not exploited until the end of the nineteenth century. The ore was transformed into lime used in the manufacture of paper pulp. For fifty years (1897 to 1945) the Tremblay family extracted it from limestone they burned in three kilns built directly on the calcite vein and loaded from the top. The lime was then transported on barges to Rivière-du-Loup. Located in Grande-Anse hollow, east of Moulin-Baude, this historic site can be visited by a trail that starts at the Maison des Dunes or by sea kayak.

The Price
era

As reported in 1872, by journalist James MacPherson Lemoine, the Kingdom of Saguenay once had a monarch:

"**This king** is the Hon. David Price, senator, great landowner and great industrialist. No sooner has one set foot on the Saguenay jetty at Anse-à-l'Eau than one is told the wharf is owned by Mr. Price. And the superb villa across from it? It belongs to Mr. Price! And the mill? Mr. Price! And the steamboat called Le Tadoussac? Mr. Price! And these lovely farms, and these white-sailed schooners all along the shore? Mr. Price! And the huge Hôtel de Tadoussac? It belongs to Mr. Price, or his employees or friends [...] With debts to collect up and down the shore, and great liberality with his debtors, the Hon. Senator has become a true power in his kingdom; of course, if anything could help one forget a monopoly, it is the savvy of the one who implements it."

James MacPherson Le Moine,
L'Album du touriste, **1872**

STARTING IN 1838, when revolt was fomenting among francophones in Lower Canada and a group called "La Société des Vingt-et-Un" attacked the Hudson Bay Company's monopoly on the King's Domain by forcing colonization in the Saguenay, Tadoussac temporarily found a new vocation: forestry.

Magnate William Price, who financed colonization in the Saguenay so as to lay hold of new territories to exploit, also laid hold of Tadoussac with the construction of a sawmill in Anse-à-l'Eau.

This period corresponded with a significant growth phase for Tadoussac and, one could say, with the forming of a real village. That is why all the oldest houses date from the beginning of what was called "The Price era", around 1838, or a subsequent era of expansion that began around 1860 with William Price's nephew, David-Edouard.

The impact of forestry on mid 19th century Tadoussac also explains one of the striking traits of the landscape at that time: the absence of trees and total barrenness of the surrounding heights. The Price enterprise had carried out a systematic harvesting of the great white pines that even Jacques Cartier had commented upon: "[…] There we saw trees as could mast a ship of thirty tonnes […]". These giants of the Saguenay shores were used to make masts or lumber sent to Great Britain from the wharf at Anse-à-l'Eau.

Hôtel Georges

The Hôtel Georges is probably the oldest building in Tadoussac, dating back to about 1838, when the sawmill was established in Anse-à-l'Eau. However, the oldest document that makes reference to it is a bill of sale signed in 1864 by David-Edouard Price and Alexandre Urqhuart.

It is said that Price managers could supervise mill workers from the second storey window.

The building has undergone several transformations that have altered its original cachet, but its distinct character has nonetheless been preserved, along with the mouldings and stair banister in the front hall.

Harold
and
Pamela Price.

104

PRICE

The Price houses

Harold Price
is a descendant of William
and David Price,
who founded
the village around the Anse-à-l'Eau sawmill in 1838.
All over Tadoussac and Saguenay–Lac-Saint-Jean
they are familiarly called "the Prices": members
of a dynasty that has made its mark on the Kingdom
of Saguenay like true monarchy. Harold Price,
a retired forestry engineer and son of the Saguenay,
embodies the strength and determination
of this family of giants whose history is inextricably
linked to the forest.

Starting in 1860, the Prices built several
houses of similar architecture that would
be sold and transformed, or simply disap-
pear.

In the Anse-à-l'Eau sector, three little
wood houses appear on period photos.
The Beattie and Molson houses, next to the
Hôtel Georges, are perfectly evocative of
this period, having barely been altered.

Other magnificent, more refined exam-
ples of Price constructions can be found in
the village.

Since his retirement he has occupied the famous
"pilot's house" built in the early 1870s by the chief
pilot on the Saguenay, Eugène Boulanger.

The Côté house

The Côté house (1865) has retained all its charm despite numerous additions, including that of the old village post office. The Côté family has inhabited the house since 1893.

The Ferguson house

Off the tourist track and inside the village, the Ferguson house was built in 1875 by the Deschênes forefathers, distinguished craftsmen whom we can thank for several houses in Tadoussac.

The Hovington house

The splendid Hovington house is a magnificent example of francophone ownership and its particular touches, especially with regard to winterization, decor and colours used in interior design.

The birth
of tourism

The lake and village of Anse-à-l'Eau,
seen from the heights of the Le Fjord trail.

SINCE THE EARLY NINETEENTH CENTURY, the modest population of Tadoussac has seen a great influx of visitors, a new type of traveler brought by the prosperity of the industrial era.

The notion of vacation was born and the resort town was developed, along with the first organized tours and necessary hospitality infrastructures. Tadoussac acquired a new vocation: tourism.

To this day, a visit to Tadoussac is not only a voyage back in time to an important part of North American history; it is not just hiking along one-of-a-kind trails or observing the noble marine mammals... Above all, it is a seemingly everlasting rendezvous with majesty and mystery.

Up until the mid nineteenth century, Whites and Natives of Tadoussac lived off the resources of sea and forest. However, these were rapidly depleted, and in the autumn of 1848, the whine of saws fell silent in the mill owned by British magnate William Price.

Then came the arrival of those Father Babel called "this crowd of foreigners".

La Presse journalist James MacPherson Lemoine, in his 1872 *Album du Touriste*, relates this glorious episode in the history of Tadoussac and takes a trip back in time:

"To speak of Tadoussac is to go back to the birthplace of our history. A trading post in America frequented by Europeans in the early sixteenth century, is in itself interesting, not only for our compatriots in Canada, but for all those who inhabit this western hemisphere, discovered by Christopher Colombus eight years before that century began.

On September 1, 1535, Cartier landed at Tadoussac. [...] In 1865, a group of our fellow citizens, high up in the business world, the Hon. D. E. Price, MM J. B. Forsyth, Wm. Rhodes, John Gilmour, Willis Russell, of Quebec City; Dr. George W. Campbell, Chs J. Brydges, Alex Urquhart, of Montreal; Jos Radford, of Tadoussac, with a capital of $40,000, organized a company to operate sea baths from a large hotel, under the name of Tadoussac Hotel and Sea Bathing Company.

In the fair season, Tadoussac sees tourists from all over the world gather in the lounges of its great hotel. The site is delectable. Some have even built themselves elegant villas, including Colonel Rhodes, Mr. Powell, of Philadelphia, Mr. Willis Russell, Mr. Jas. L. Gibb, Mr. Price, Mr. J. Gilmour, of Quebec, Mr. Radford, of Tadoussac."

In 1860, Tadoussac had a population of two hundred, most of whom came from Charlevoix. Businessman John Lord had already built a hotel on the point at Anse-à-l'Eau, on the Saguenay side of the village.

The trademark of the establishment was therapeutic fresh and salt water bathing, "of great virtue for curing dyspepsia", it was said.

In 1864, with the tourist population ever increasing, construction began on the Hôtel Tadoussac. The arrival of the first cruise liners on the St. Lawrence and Saguenay gave tourism in Tadoussac a considerable boost, confirming its vocation as a tourist attraction, then as a resort town, when rich American and Canadian businessmen started building their villas there.

"Tadoussac, writes journalist, M. J. C. Taché, sits like a nest amongst the granite rocks surrounding the Saguenay river mouth. The chapel and post houses occupy the edge of a pretty plateau atop a steep dune that curves around a charming little bay. Thus perched, the buildings overlook a narrow shore of fine sand. To the right, one's view plunges down into the depths of the dark Saguenay; ahead, it is lost in the immense St. Lawrence. All around are mountains covered with woods of fir trees and silver birches. Through the opening the powerful river has forged through the rock, we see the strand, islands and South Shore of the Great St. Lawrence. It is a delicious place."

It is fascinating to see how these descriptions, written 125 years ago, still hold true in so many ways.

Hôtel Tadoussac

In the middle of the panoramic view of Tadoussac stands the famous Hôtel Tadoussac, a major and incontrovertible fixture. The first hotel, built in 1868 and fully overhauled in 1888, was demolished in 1941. The hotel as it is today was constructed by a key personality: William-Hugh Coverdale, president of Canada Steamship Lines.

This brilliant and cultivated shipowner, a lover of art and antique furniture, made the Hôtel Tadoussac the institution it is today. The many cruise boats anchored in Tadoussac Bay ensured local prosperity until 1966, when the "white ships" ceased to operate. The hotel began to deteriorate but was taken over by the Dufour family of Isle-aux-Coudres, a group of ship and hotel owners based in eastern Quebec who successfully relaunched tourism by developing large-scale whale watching along the river, as well as cruises on the fjord.

The splendid hotel, where the film **Hotel New Hampshire** was shot, still represents the soul of the landscape and nerve centre of tourist activity. However, the village also offers a variety of little inns, restaurants and a campground that greatly complements the accommodations structure, and blends harmoniously with the atmosphere and general setting of this magnificent little tourist haven that is Tadoussac.

The Hôtel Tadoussac...

... over a century of history

Center: the hotel circa 1865. Below, left: the staff circa 1960.

The Dufferin house

In 1872, when the Governor General of Canada, Lord Dufferin, acquired the land on which he built his summer residence, Tadoussac became the focus of the entire northeastern aristocracy. What an extraordinary promotion for this new vacation spot!

Inspired by British colonial manors in India, the Dufferin villa was built in sections in Quebec then transported by river to Tadoussac, where it was assembled. Today it belongs to the Smith family.

site, built in 1873, and was inhabited by Mr. Fletcher, military secretary to Lord Dufferin, Governor General of Canada. The original building was sold to the Prices in 1878, and rebuilt in 1897 by Mrs. Amelia Price. Since then, descendants of the family have summered there.

The Fletcher house

The Price family occupied this magnificent bayside residence for over a century. Before that, another house stood on the

A new phenomenon

Towards the mid nineteenth century, industrialization would bring profound changes to life in North America. There was a mass move towards cities and terrible epidemics spread through the unsanitary urban sprawl. The bourgeoisie flourished and a new social stratum appeared: the middle class. The idea of summer vacations in the country became popular among families who could afford them. People also fled the cities to get away from diseases by which rural areas remain untouched.

According to popular philosophy of that time, idleness was the source of all vice and numerous physical weaknesses. A sojourn at Tadoussac in a spirit of transhumance helped break the routine. It provided a pleasant change of scene with a new and less hierarchical social order, and inspired a new art de vivre in reaction to the frenzy of modern life. It was the birth of what would become a real social phenomenon, and then a major industry: tourism.

At that time, and up until the next century, visitors would be lodged with local families, at least in Charlevoix. In Tadoussac it was different; wealthier visitors lived in their own villas, whereas others took advantage of the hotels.

But even in holiday time, the social hierarchy was pronounced and good manners were essential. Children were not bound by the rules of society, but adults had to stay within their ranks.

As for those whom the locals called "sportsmen" or "gentlemen", they took leave of their families to practice the "sport of kings": salmon fishing on the Sainte-Marguerite and other big salmon rivers of the North Shore.

Daily life was divided between golf and the beach, croquet and tennis, picnics and teatime, photography and watercolour-painting. These activities were the essence of what was called "St. Lawrence summer life".

What A.B. Routhier said of Pointe-au-Pic in 1881 could also have been said of Tadoussac:

"It is the favourite retreat of city people fleeing the heat and dust of the city. It is a meeting place for those who wish to cool

Sportsmen and gentlemen practise the sport of kings on nearby rivers.

off and rest their limbs in the waters of the bay, smell the kelp, the salty breath of the sea and the fragrant breeze from the resinous woods that crown the mountaintops."

This was the beginning of a wave of prosperity for Tadoussac, and a large part of its economic development became centred on tourism, the hotel business, sea transport and outdoor activities.

Tadoussac: the English way

It is possible to visit Tadoussac without really noticing the presence of its summer anglophones. It is possible to think one knows Tadoussac just because one has been going there for years, yet without knowing anything about this community that has summered there for one and a half century.

One may just know there are villas in Tadoussac and that they belong to English people. However, it is very exciting to discover this society of Tadoussac devotees, these families who have played such a key role in the history of the village.

The anglophones who chose Tadoussac as their summer home built cottages, in some cases architecturally daring but for the most part plain, with a rustic or peasant style. Stone constructions are rare, as are luxurious buildings built as status symbols.

The favoured material is wood, Tadoussac's second raison-d'être. Warm materials such as cedar or pine from the old Price sawmills were left to age untreated, taking on the gentle nuances of the years.

Some of the interiors have been brightened up with colours like brilliant yellow, rich green, and majestic ochre that give depth to the villas of Parc Languedoc.

In the village are more traditional-looking villas, built by the Price family from 1838 on, to which a number of extensions, enlargements and other modifications were added around 1860.

What the members of the anglophone community have in common is an unshakable sense of belonging towards this little piece of paradise they chose years ago for its charming atmosphere, fresh air and, at that time, its tranquillity.

It seems the residents of Parc Languedoc and the shore feel a little apart from the villagers, being more inclined to social activities such as five o'clock tea, tennis and golf. Parc Languedoc residents prefer

their peace and quiet, neigh-
bourly relations, and a truly
spectacular landscape.

But no matter! The
English stick together and
fiercely protect their lifestyle,
religion, habits and culture.
They maintain what they
have acquired over the generations, knowing that time
and life pass more slowly
here than in other places.

Children can still run to
the store to buy candy, hide
in the maze of trails, play hide-and-seek in
attics and spend the afternoon at the pool
or beach.

Every Friday afternoon, the adults get
together at the tennis club. Sunday
morning, the Anglican chapel bell calls the
faithful to the 10:30 service, a fervent
ceremony indeed.

The gathering outside the church after
the service is a very civil event, in which
the pastor is surrounded by his flock, from

children to the elderly. It is the only time
that tourists can see these people gathered
in plain view before returning to their own
summer milieu.

We meet only the warmest and most
welcoming people in this group, people with
a fantastic heritage and extraordinary
memories who are terribly happy to have
their place in Tadoussac. It is clear that without them, Tadoussac would not be the same,
its historical patrimony not quite so rich.

The Anglican chapel

At the Anglican chapel, surrounded by big trees, the English community of Tadoussac meets each week in summer for the Sunday service. Built in 1867, the chapel depends on the sponsorship of each English family for its upkeep.

Each detail of the chapel furnishings and decor evokes the longstanding tradition and belonging of Tadoussac's anglophone families. Pretty and discreet, the chapel also evokes the devotion of these people, and their deep gratitude for the privilege of spending their summers in a place as extraordinary as Tadoussac.

Parc Languedoc

Parc Languedoc is not a park or public place, but an old vacation domain now hidden away in the woods. During the 1920s the shrewish Madame Jones-Languedoc, whom author Benny Beattie nicknamed "the witch of the woods", reigned over the place in such a memorable manner that her name has remained associated with this group of peaceful villas to which several modern châteaux have been added since 1998.

The Bailey house

Considered one of the most remarkable villas in Tadoussac, the Bailey house has been occupied by the Bailey family since 1930. It was built in 1865, in the style of the Bardsville salmon fishing club on the Sainte-Marguerite River, and was first owned by Robert Hare Powell, a club member.

The O'Neil house

This wood cottage of squared timber, built around 1900, inherited a colourful history, having been demolished, moved and rebuilt two times. In the doorway: Mrs. Elizabeth O'Neil.

Amberly

Mrs Languedoc's summer residence for 75 years. She called it "Amberly", claiming to be related on her mother's side to the Duke of Bedford, owner of Amberly castle in England.

Parc Languedoc

The Turcot house

Hector Gauthier and Henri-Paul Hovington built this superb villa in 1948 from the blueprints of architect Frank Morewood, replicating the Dutch-style design of his own Philadelphia home.

Tivoli

First owned by Madame Adèle Languedoc, the house was purchased in 1918 by Professor Robert McLean of the University of Rochester, New York, who called it "Tivoli" in memory of a European idyll.

The Tudor-Hart house

The villa has an extraordinary view of the bay and was built in 1922 by Godfrey Rhodes of Quebec, then inhabited after 1936 by his daughter and her husband, the well-known painter Perceval Tudor-Hart. Today it is owned by Benny and Gita Beattie.

Spruce Cliff

The three Stevenson sisters: Elizabeth, Ann and Margaret.

Top right: Three generations of vacationers on the balcony of the Spruce Cliff villa, a jewel among Tadoussac's heritage buidings, dating from 1861: The O'Neils, Dewarts and Reilleys: Elizabeth, Katherine, Brian; Ann, Margaret, Prudence, Judy, Beth, Jonah and Callie.

La Soupière (the Soupery)

This villa, whose construction was completed in 1924, was so named because of its unusual colour.
The charming ladies of the house greatly add to its appeal.
On the front porch: Mrs. Dewart and Mrs. Elliot.

The little yacht *Le Noroît* passes a cruise boat entering Tadoussac.

The white ships

They were called **Saguenay**, **Magnet**, **Montréal**, **Québec**, **Union**, **St. Lawrence**, **Canada**, **Richelieu**; they sailed for The Richelieu and Ontario Navigation Co. or Canada Steamship Lines, offered excursions to the end of the Saguenay fjord, with departures from Quebec and Montreal. They were the "white ships", cruise ships whose every arrival at the Tadoussac wharf was an event. People ran to watch them sail in, and see elegant ladies and dapper men emerge. These floating buildings had an air of dignity and richesse: paddleboats and small steamships, designed especially for the St. Lawrence, that proudly sailed the waters of Tadoussac Bay until 1965.

These cruise boats represented the ultimate in tourism at

a time when vacation trends were just being invented. The public was charmed by the luxury of the vast lounges, munificent woodwork, extraordinary service, genteel atmosphere and warm Victorian decor, which even the most difficult patrons found irresistible.

Journalist and columnist Arthur Buies was one of the most fervent travelers of his day. He who had travelled from one end of Quebec to the other, wrote in his **Petites chroniques pour 1877**:

"Tell me what aperitif is worth one hour at sunrise on the deck of the **Union** or the **Saguenay** as the day star climbs higher and higher above the horizon, flooding nature with its light though without yet embracing it, and when the aromatic air, pure and hearty, rushes into one's avid lungs and gasping gullets! Tell me what pleasure, what joy is worth this drunkenness of the senses, a peaceful and fortifying drunkenness that enters every pore, ripples

Cruise boat at the Tadoussac wharf circa 1965.

through every fibre and fills the entire soul! Ah, sometimes God is good to His miserable creature, and the St. Lawrence company deserves all the transports of our gratitude! "

Pleasure cruises on the St. Lawrence began around 1830 with the **Waterloo**, owned by John Molson's St. Lawrence Steamboat Company.

From 1853 on, the Saguenay fjord became the destination of choice for cruises on the steamship **Saguenay**, owned by the Quebec and Trois-Pistoles Steam Navigation Company of which William Price was one of ten shareholders. Tadous-

The *St. Lawrence.*

sac was naturally a high point in the three-day tour out of Quebec City, which at that time cost $12. At the Anse-à-l'Eau wharf where the ferryboats arrive today, then at the federal wharf, "calèches" awaited passengers to take them on a tour of the village or to the Hôtel Tadoussac. The steamship then continued on its way to the fjord, an unforgettable experience for some passengers.

A columnist from **Harper's Magazine** reported:

"I have stood in the presence of the Niagara, and there regarded the voice of man as sacrilegious impertinence: but never have I felt the insignificance of human utterance and human effort as when standing still in the presence of those silent preachers of omnipotence, capes Trinity and Eternity, with the broad evens above filled with the light and the unstable waters below deep and black, where darkness eternally broods. It was a lesson of humility long to be remembered."

"**Food** on board is remarkably good and varied, and what's more, things are made with elegance and a sort of abundance that to my mind is the most flattering compliment one can pay the passengers."

Arthur Buies, *Petites chroniques pour 1877*

83

In 1857, the Compagnie du Richelieu was created, and the legendary steamship **Québec** emerged some years later from the shipyard at Sorel. It was followed by the **Union**, the **Clyde**, the **Saguenay**, **Tadoussac**, **Richelieu** and **St. Lawrence**, names that remain etched on the memories of the Tadoussac people.

In 1913, the shipowning companies merged to form the giant Canada Steamship Lines which operated the "white ships" up until the mid 1960s.

Today, we still see some of their immense modern-day descendants pass Tadoussac and enter the Saguenay river estuary, but with foreign flags on their flagpoles.

The Richelieu

The most prestigious of the four Canada Steamship Lines ships that crossed the

On the afternoon of August 14, 1950 the *Québec* was heading for the Tadoussac wharf when thick smoke started pouring from its upper deck.

In the distance, the shrilling plaint of sirens could be heard, gradually dying away, as if they were out of breath.

The 480 passengers and 150 crew members escaped the fire, a work of arson still vividly remembered by Tadoussac residents and summer visitors.

The *Jacques-Cartier*.

waters off Tadoussac was the **Richelieu**. Stocked with provisions for a one-week cruise, it left every Monday from the Victoria dock in the Port of Montreal with 200 passengers aboard, including entire families of vacationers with luggage and car. The boat docked at Anse-à-l'Eau every Wednesday and spent the night there. The village celebrated with a gigantic campfire, music, dancing, and outdoor meals.

The ferries

The ferries that link the shores of the Saguenay river mouth are an integral part of Tadoussac heritage. Though some deplore the long waits, the ferry provides a unique opportunity to contemplate the majesty of the Saguenay and St. Lawrence. But the crossing has not always been so easy.

In the nineteenth century, powerful currents and menacing ice floes had to be navigated by canoe. Then around 1900, the Price company organized a mail transport and the job was taken on by several other boats until 1927. The first regular service was introduced with the **Pixie B**, then the MV **Jacques-Cartier** in 1938, linking Tadous-sac to the wharf at Baie-Sainte-Catherine, a much longer trip than it is today.

From 1958 on, the ferryboats started to expand with the NM **Saguenay** which could transport 21 vehicles and 200 passengers. The NM **Charlevoix** transported 21 cars in 1959. In 1974, the **Pierre de Saurel** joined the fleet to reply to the demands of truck transport. With the significant increase in car and truck traffic, the Société des Traversiers du Québec launched two new ships in 1980: the **Jos Deschênes** and the **Armand Imbeau**, thus consolidating an extremely important local economic activity.

The idea of building a bridge on the Saguenay has been under debate for several years, but it will be a long time before the ferry signal ceases to be heard in Tadoussac

Giants
of the estuary

For some years, the whales of the St. Lawrence estuary have been stealing the spotlight from the most famous tourist attraction in Quebec.

This is a recent phenomenon, for it wasn't until the beginning of the 1980s that the first whale watching "excursions" were offered. For two dollars, you could set out by rowboat, sometimes doing the rowing, to see these strange creatures that visit the waters off Tadoussac.

The names Henri Otis and Levis Ross were associated with the first real whale excursions, which left from Les Bergeronnes.

Starting in 1982, the Société linéenne de Québec, with its boat the **Samuel-de-Champlain**, laid the foundations for what would become a veritable ecotourist industry.

Since that time tourists have flocked to Tadoussac from all over the world, and now several dozen ships and a variety of smaller boats take them out to discover marine mammals.

The whale most often seen in the Tadoussac/Les Escoumins sector is the finback whale, a twenty-six metre giant (30 to 80 tons). Small rorquals are often sighted too (9.8 metres for males, 11 metres for females). Even the smallest of them, formerly called "Gibar", weighs up to ten tons. This joyful and solitary little whale often approaches the boats or shore, and regularly swims into Tadoussac Bay. Its oversized head is 40% the size of its whole body.

As for the beluga, or white whale, it is quite regularly seen in the Saguenay and St. Lawrence. There are still about 700 of them, and the pod is protected because it is considered endangered.

The luckiest ecotourists will see the blue whale, the most impressive animal to have evolved on this earth: up to 33 metres long and weighing 190 tons. A striking example of its great size: its main stomach can hold up to 1,000 tons of water and food. Sometimes, due to stiffness, the blue whale throws its tail up in the air before diving down underwater, a breath-taking spectacle much sought after by connaisseurs.

The humpback whale, which raises its tail with every dive or leaps out of the water, rarely appears in the mouth of the fjord, but in the past few seasons has been sighted more often, sometimes in large groups. The same goes for the mysterious sperm whale. Some individual sperm whales return almost annually, like the famous Tryphon. Seals are often seen, as well as entire schools of white-flanked dolphins.

A wide variety of vessels take tourists out to discover the great marine mammals. The most spacious of them can accommodate over 600 passengers, and certain outboards as few as a dozen. Those who seek strong sensations will prefer the quick and safe inflatables. Those who seek comfort but do not want to miss anything will choose the big boats, which are just as effective. Naturalist guides are on hand to comment, providing useful information and creating an environmental context for the spectacle.

What do you see? First of all, whale breath: a jet of condensation in the distance, rising into the air as the whale exhales on reaching the surface. Next, it dives underwater for several minutes, down among the schools of krill and foraging fish it so loves to eat. Whales generally stay at the surface a few instants and blow three or four times before plunging again. We see their huge impressive form, then the blowhole opening, and hear the powerful whistle before the animal rounds its back and returns to the depths of its undersea world.

A rich milieu

The whales spend spring and summer in the lower St. Lawrence because it is one of the world's richest sectors in terms of krill and small crustaceans, which the great mammals ingest by the ton. The very cold currents that follow the gradual rise in the seabed, which starts at Les Escoumins, bring to the surface an exceptionally dense population of vegetable plankton that increases exponentially upon contact with oxygen and light, in turn feeding an exceptionally dense population of animal plankton.

This is what attracts the baleen whale and other animals to this place: the inexhaustible food supply.

A threat?

Recent research conducted by GREMM (the Groupe de recherche et d'éducation sur le milieu marin), in collaboration with the Saguenay–St. Lawrence Marine Park and Fisheries and Oceans Canada, has allowed us to establish the daily routine of finback whales and observe that whales can be disturbed by too many boats. The presence of boats leads them to spend less time catching their breath, which means they cannot stay underwater long enough to get sufficient food.

It is difficult to predict whether this disturbance will have medium and long-term repercussions on the health and behaviour of whales, but these findings nonetheless allow us to envisage ways in which the whales and also the tourist industry can be protected.

Porpoise hunters on the pointe de l'Islet.

Jacques Cartier meets the belugas

"The next day, in the morning, we hoisted the sails and cast off;

and we encountered a sort of fish neither seen nor heard tell of by man.

These fish are greater than porpoise, without scales, and their bodies

and heads are the shape of a hare's, white as snow with no marks;

and there are many such fish in the said river, and they live between

the sea and fresh water The people of that country call them «adhothuys»;

and they say they are very good to eat, and affirmed that this animal

is to be found in no other place in this river or this country."

Jacques Cartier, 3 September 1535

The case of the beluga

Swimming by Tadoussac Bay, they seem joyful, happy, carefree. However, the surviving beluga pods in the lower St. Lawrence and the Saguenay have been decimated by the hunt and today are threatened by pollution.

For centuries, these toothed whales were pursued by whalers for their fat, and by fishermen who blamed them for ruining their business. The government even offered a bounty for their capture.

The population had collapsed to such a degree that the hunt was outlawed, and the St. Lawrence beluga was put on the list of endangered species. For a long time, census counts showed no significant growth in the livestock, which remained stagnant at about 500 individuals.

However, recent figures point to an increase in the population, which is now at about 700. Still, several belugas are washed up every year, fatally poisoned by invertebrates: eels or mollusks they have ingested from polluted places in the seabed. Moreover, belugas live in isolation, without contact with the Beaufort Sea population, and face serious problems of inbreeding, which weakens their genetic makeup. Their maximum life span is thirty years, with the young reaching maturity at seven years. In summer the beluga population is distributed over a large portion of the lower St. Lawrence and most of the Saguenay fjord.

They are regularly sighted in the waters off Tadoussac, but it is forbidden to approach them, since it was established that the presence of pleasure or observation boats affect their behaviour.

93

A natural
environment
to protect

The Saguenay–St. Lawrence Marine Park

THE ECOLOGICAL MILIEU of Tadoussac Bay being particularly complex and fragile, it encompasses two parks: the Saguenay–St. Lawrence Marine Park, under federal–provincial jurisdiction, and the Parc du Saguenay, under Quebec provincial jurisdiction.

Tadoussac Bay is right in the heart of Quebec's first marine park. Its territory covers most of the Saguenay fjord bed to the edge of the cape, to the east, and up to the middle of the St. Lawrence estuary, from Les Escoumins to Gros-cap-à-l'Aigle, near Saint-Fidèle. This zone includes the marine ecosystems on and off Tadoussac, in Charlevoix, off Pointe-Noire and Baie-Sainte-Catherine, Saint-Siméon, Port-au-Persil, Port-au-Saumon and Saint-Fidèle. Located at the confluence of the St. Lawrence estuary and Saguenay fjord, both Tadoussac and Pointe-Noire are ideal places from which to observe the merging of major water masses and the passage of beluga whales.

The Saguenay–St. Lawrence Marine Park is the first marine conservation area in Quebec, with a surface area of 1,138 km². It has the mandate of protecting and promoting a significant part of the St. Lawrence estuary and Saguenay fjord.

The Saguenay–St. Lawrence Marine Park has many unique qualities, including the very nature of its territory, an open system that essentially consists of water and ends at the high water point. The project of creating Quebec's first marine park was made official by the federal and provincial governments with the signing of a protocol in 1990.

Two series of public consultations were held in 1993, and three years later a master plan was drawn up, outlining the park's main objectives. The park was instituted by federal and provincial laws that were adopted in 1997 and announced in the summer of 1998.

The Tadoussac wharf and those of other nearby villages became departure points for numerous marine mammal observation excursions. Marine park management conducted research on these activities and drafted an ethical code in collaboration with those working in the milieu, in order to ensure the sustainability of the resource and the observation tours. We also know that Tadoussac and Baie-Sainte-Catherine were instrumental settings in the history of First Nation/ European contact. The rest of the territory represents an integral part of the beluga habitat, as well as a well-travelled navigation route.

The Saguenay–St. Lawrence Marine Park allows for joint management of these ecosystems and renewable resources, with the aim of preserving biological diversity, the integrity of ecosystems and cultural witnesses.

The organization's primary mandate is the preservation of marine ecosystems and

Observation from the shores of Cap-de-Bon-Désir.

the well-being of riverside residents who have always lived in symbiosis with the sea. This concern is translated into research and initiatives aimed at better understanding marine mammals in the St. Lawrence estuary and how their behaviour is affected by observation activities. This mandate also extends to the establishment of partnerships with the milieu, hospitality structures, boat access and discovery circuits.

Federal offices for the Saguenay–St. Lawrence Marine Park are located in Tadoussac, and the Parcs Québec offices in Ville de La Baie.

Cap-de-Bon-Désir

The Centre d'interprétation et d'observation de Cap-de-Bon-Désir is an incomparable location from which to observe marine mammals from dry land. It is also an ideal place to spend a pleasant day near the lighthouse, communing with shore life and waiting for the whales to come play by the water's edge, as is their habit. It is also an exceptionally fertile archaeological site with a fascinating interpretive centre staffed by naturalist guides from the Explo Nature organization and the Corporation touristique de Bergeronnes.

Pointe-Noire

The Centre d'interprétation et d'observation de Pointe-Noire, on the Baie-Sainte-Catherine side, is staffed by the team from GREMM (Groupe de recherche et d'éducation sur le milieu marin) and Explo Nature. Together they help visitors discover, admire and understand the oceanographic phenomena that unfold in the complex environment of the Saguenay fjord. The promontory provides a striking viewpoint from which groups of belugas can often be seen entering the Saguenay.

Belugas can be regularly seen from the lookouts of the Pointe-Noire interpretation and observation centre.

Parc du Saguenay

Officially created in June 1983 by the government of Quebec, the Parc du Saguenay has for many years generated public interest in the protection and promotion of this rich territory. The park was developed along with surrounding communities including Tadoussac.

Parc du Saguenay has the status of a conservation park and is representative of the Saguenay fjord area.

Parc du Saguenay is also known as one of the most beautiful hiking spots in the eastern North American continent.

Devotees of short, medium and long distance hiking can choose from trails and shelters on both shores of the Saguenay that offer sublime views of the fjord and untamed nature of this mountainous land.

There are three entry points or poles of interest on park territory, the main one located at Rivière-Éternité. The welcome centre for the Tadoussac sector, located in the Maison des Dunes, provides information on park activities and offers an interpretive exhibit on the Saguenay, glaciations and special features of the dunes sector.

The most recently developed welcome centre is at Baie-Sainte-Marguerite and specializes in the interpretation of the beluga. The **Le Fjord** hiking trail, which runs along the North Shore of

Taking a break on the trails of Saguenay Park.

because the big neo-colonial residence was built in 1922 by Noël Brisson, who supervised the neighbouring sawmill and power plant. The house, which has a spectacular view, was acquired by Colin J. C. Molson in 1962 and by the government of Quebec in 1984.

Hiking

The **Le Fjord** trail links Tadoussac to Baie Sainte-Marguerite. It offers breathtaking views of the fjord and fjord mouth, and the village and bay of Tadoussac. It takes four days to do the whole trail, sleeping in a shelter or under the stars. On a one-day hike, hikers normally complete the section between Anse de la Boule (Sacré-Cœur) and the village of Tadoussac, which offers many beautiful panoramic views. Connaisseurs say it is one of the most remarkable hiking trails in Quebec and all of northeastern North America.

In the heart of the village are two short trails that include interpretive plaques. The trails, **La-colline-de-l'Anse-à-l'Eau** and **La-pointe-de-l'Islet**, reveal the fascinating secrets of nature in the place where fjord and river meet.

Saguenay Park Interpretation centre (Maison des Dunes).

the Saguenay from the Anse-à-l'Eau sector, leads all the way to Baie Sainte-Marguerite.

Parc du Saguenay has been twinned with Parc des Cévennes in France since 1984.

Maison des Dunes

The Parc du Saguenay interpretive centre is also referred to as "Maison Brisson"

Trails that offer striking
views or extend along
the great river's shore.

Opposite: *Le Fjord* trail;
Below: *La-colline-de-l'Anse-à-l'Eau*
trail.

Promenade on the pointe de l'Islet.

La pointe de l'Islet

The Islet peninsula, shared by the Saguenay and Tadoussac Bay, is uninhabited today, except for a few villas at its inland end. Once the exclusive territory of the Hudson Bay Company, the peninsula was taken over by a group of self-proclaimed Native squatters during the second half of the nineteenth century. About eighteen families of hunters and fishermen lived there, Montagnais on the Saguenay side and Metis on the bay side, until the hotel took possession of the rock and expelled its occupants, on account (so it claimed) of the odours produced by the transformation of fishing and hunting products.

The **La Plage** or beach trail, which links the village to the dune sector, allows for a close view of the littoral split, both rock and sand, and magnificent views of the St. Lawrence estuary. It is not a precisely outlined trail but a seaside hiking path that can only be accessed at low tide.

The **circuit patrimonial** (heritage circuit), which goes through the streets of Tadoussac, reveals important historical highlights of the little coastal village. The circuit takes us, for example, to Cale sèche (dry dock), a unique historical site where Tadoussac craftsmen once developed their local specialty as builders of small boats and schooners. The dry dock doors still open today, at high tide in fall and spring, for the storage of boats over the winter.

take advantage of the equipment and services of the Marina de Tadoussac, located at the heart of the action and providing a front-row view of a truly captivating natural and human spectacle.

The Tadoussac marina

The Tadoussac Bay sector is known for its top-notch nautical facilities. Sailing and water-sports lovers can

Some kayakers even head out to sea to watch the whales, unaware of the dangers that make such adventures inadvisable.

Golf

Indissociable from English tradition, the Hôtel Tadoussac golf club remains one of the favourite recreation sites for the holiday community, and is also open to tourists and residents. The nine hole, par 31, 2,133-yard course has preserved its unique, relaxed and rustic character in a lovely natural setting.

The tennis club

What could be more British than "five o'clock tea"? This custom has remained very much alive among the holiday community in Tadoussac and is inextricably associated with the picturesque tennis club, built in 1912 next to the golf course. To this day, the three courts serve as an arena for duels between top players in all categories, dressed in the traditional de rigueur white. Every Friday in July and August, summer residents meet there to watch the match, chat, drink tea and eat the delicious snacks prepared by the ladies of the organizing committee.

Sea kayaking

Sea kayak devotees have also adopted Tadoussac Bay as a first-choice destination for practising their sublime sport.

The estuaries are particularly rough and dangerous in this type of vessel, but for kayakers who glide quietly over smoother waters, the east shore of the St. Lawrence from Tadoussac Bay to Grande-Anse has many wonders in store: flocks of sea birds around Caye-à-Edgar, the splendour of the dunes seen from the water, the fluctuating sea currents of the Pointe-aux-Vaches strand, the occasional appearance of little rorqual or beluga whale off Rochers-du-Saguenay, the waterfall in the river at Moulin-à-Baude and the chowdowns on the shore or rocks of Caye-à-Quenon, to name just a few.

The campground

Tadoussac is blessed with one of the loveliest campgrounds one can imagine. No other campground offers such an impressive view, which overlooks the village, the Saguenay river mouth and St. Lawrence estuary. This environment in perpetual movement is a riveting spectacle and an incomparable asset for the Camping Tadoussac, whose popularity is more than justified.

More birds than meet the eye...

Amateur ornithologists watching the banks of the Saguenay are often amazed by the rarity or even absence of winged fauna. "These are real deserts, inhabitable by beast or bird", wrote Champlain. This is due in great part to the steep cliffs, the littoral split and lack of vegetation for food or shelter. It must be recognized that

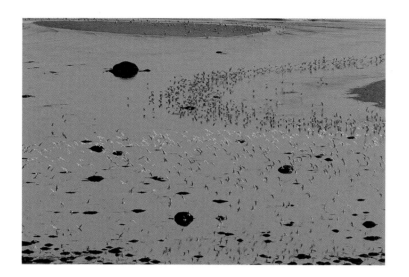

From eiders to gulls

Over 25,000 eider duck couples nest in the St. Lawrence estuary, especially on Ile Rouge. Their population is relatively stable though the species is very sought after by hunters.

After nesting season, an interesting transhumance occurs whereby the eiders of the estuary and Gulf of St. Lawrence leave to spend the winter on the shores of Nova Scotia and New England, and are replaced by eiders from Labrador and Ungava who come spend the cold season in "the South", mainly around the Mingan archipelago.

Next, Ile Rouge goes to the gulls, who literally take it over and conduct a devastating siege. The herring gull is particularly

Saguenay bird life is one of the least documented aspects of the fjord. A count conducted by the Saguenay amateur birdwatchers in the Rivière-Éternité and Tadoussac sectors made it possible to enumerate 161 species of birds in 41 families and about 17,000 migrations of birds of prey. The Saguenay river mouth is considered a prime wintering spot; in autumn and winter, ten thousand birds per linear kilometre take advantage of this ice-free zone, mostly aquatic birds, including a high concentration of ducks (mainly black ducks and eiders).

present on Ile Rouge in both summer and winter. The Quebec population is estimated at 45,000 couples. This represents a considerable increase over the last decade, now on the decline due to the drastic drop in fish remains, which before the moratoria on commercial fishing were thrown into the sea.

Cormorants are also to be found among the gulls, as well as fleet-footed and curious redshanks, and lastly, kakawi ducks, who remain there for part of the winter.

Visiting Tadoussac

Gustave Catellier, former manager of the fish hatchery, his wife Emma and their descendants lived in this spacious residence for over 55 years before it became Tadoussac's first police station. Built in 1863, the house was given a new vocation in the 1990s when it was acquired by the North Shore tourist bureau (Maison du Tourisme de la Côte-Nord).

It is there one can find all available information and documentation on the North Shore, especially about Tadoussac, lodging, cruises, services and activities.

La Maison du Tourisme de la Côte-Nord
197, rue des Pionniers,
Tadoussac (Québec) Canada GOT 2AO
Telephone: (418) 235-4744

Centre d'interprétation des mammifères marins (CIMM)

A STAY AT TADOUSSAC is an encounter with the many vestiges of a rich history, but also with a present where all efforts have been made to reveal the secrets of a magnanimous natural environment. This is no doubt part of Tadoussac's irresistible appeal for the 250,000 or more visitors who return there year after year.

Maison du Tourisme or Maison Catellier

All visits to Tadoussac should begin with a visit to the splendid Maison du Tourisme de la Côte-Nord, formerly known as the Maison Catellier.

"Better understanding for better protection"

Tadoussac Bay is home to a very active marine research group, GREMM (Groupe de recherche et d'éducation sur le milieu marin). Founded in 1985, it is dedicated to scientific research and education on St. Lawrence marine mammals and the protection of their habitats. The innovative approach of this multidisciplinary team has led to a happy marriage of research and education, especially in its development of interpretive programmes presented by naturalists on whale watching cruise boats.

GREMM also operates the Centre d'interprétation des

mammals. Since it opened in 1991, CIMM has attracted over 30,000 visitors annually and proved its profitability within a space of three years.

Station piscicole de Tadoussac (fish hatchery)

Built in 1875 on the former premises of the Anse-à-l'Eau sawmill, the Station piscicole de Tadoussac is one of the oldest institutions of its kind in North America. Despite its long history, by the end of the 1980s this government enterprise had become one of the most modern piscicultures on the continent. Computerized water management, as well as heating and recirculation

mammifères marins (CIMM), a lively and captivating modern natural museum located near the dry dock, a treasure trove of information on the lives of marine

Fish hatchery circa nineteenth century.

Tanks at the Anse-à-l'Eau fish hatchery.

of the water makes it possible to produce Atlantic salmon twice as quickly as in traditional fish farming. These fish are raised to stock salmon rivers all over Quebec. The 600 breeding fish produce 2,000,000 eggs and 200,000 parr.

The maritime museum

The Musée maritime Molson-Beattie is a tiny but rich treasure trove of historical objects that record the great moments of navigation and shipbuilding in Tadoussac. The displays are strikingly detailed and authentic, with astounding images and an

The sailing ship *Bonne Chance*.

abundance of unusual artefacts that take us back to the days of the white ships or schooners.

However, the most impressive pieces of this collection, accumulated over the 1960s by James Beattie and Colin J. G. Molson, are stored in two barns behind the museum. There we can visit the sailing ship **Bonne Chance** in full sail. A barn has been

constructed around it, originally from Sacré-Cœur.

This nine metre "yawl" had a long navigational career on the Saguenay and St. Lawrence, sailing out of its home port, Tadoussac. Some trace its history back to 1870 whereas others say it was built on Ile-Verte in 1910.

When its sailing days were over, it was saved from dereliction and conserved as an eloquent demonstration of the craft of the old shipbuilders.

The buildings also house the old Tadoussac fire-car and sled, as well as the hearse and a calèche belonging to the Hovington family. Benny Beattie tells of how his father bought these pieces for a grand total of $35.

The brick house was built in 1865 by Evan John Price. In 1991, Mr. Molson bequeathed it and the collection to Heritage Canada of Quebec, headed by his son Robin Molson.

The Indian Chapel

After the first places of worship built in 1617, 1629 and 1661, the Indian Chapel was erected by the Jesuit Claude-Godefroi Coquart in 1747. It was used by North Shore and Lac Saint-Jean Montagnais starting June 24, 1750. Though it has been renovated several times, it is considered the oldest wooden chapel in the country.

The interior is particularly sober and contains several noteworthy objects from the period. A walk through the nearby cemetery brings one in contact with the families who made Tadoussac history.

The Chauvin trading post

It was here that it all began. Run by several trading companies, including the famous and powerful Hudson Bay Co., the Maison Chauvin remained a more or less vital trade centre from 1600 to 1859, when the fur trade collapsed and the post closed.

In 1942, William Hugues Coverdale revived Chauvin house by building an original replica, which has since displayed a collection of artefacts and historical pieces in a museum setting.

Hovington farm

Almost nothing remains of Tadoussac's agricultural past, except for Hovington farm, between the village and the dunes.

Alexandre Hovington, who had it built around 1892, was a very important agricultural producer, supplying Tadoussac with milk, vegetables, eggs and even meat at butchering time in the fall.

The farm is set back from Rue des Pionniers, and today belongs to the Quebec government. It continues to produce berries in season, and apples on a pick-your-own basis.

A sense of celebration

The Tadoussaciens, like all Québécois, know how to party. They do not miss a chance to celebrate life, friendship, and the pleasure of looking out every day on the idyllic panorama of Tadoussac Bay.

Over the past few years, outdoor terraces and cafés have sprung up, attracting residents and visitors alike. Among these, Le Gibar is considered a local institution, for it was a chosen spot for the hippies of the first wave and remains a meeting place

The Hovington farm.

for it was a chosen spot for the hippies of the first wave and remains a meeting place for human fauna of both the daytime and nighttime variety.

The fate of the world has been decided many a time in this unique building, which has no terrain and is painted a striking colour. Built in 1908, it housed one of the first village souvenir shops from 1925 to 1980.

A festival of song

In the second weekend in June, the hottest new names in Quebec music as well as numerous established artists gather in Tadoussac for a four day festival that is almost intimate, yet which has made its mark throughout Quebec.

The Festival de la chanson de Tadoussac consists of simultaneous performances in village bars and cafés, and provides an ideal pretext for launching the tourist season a few weeks early.

André Tremblay, left,
watches over
Youth Hostel visitors.

The youth hostel

If young tourists swarm to Tadoussac and onto the whale-watching boats, it is thanks to the Auberge de jeunesse de Tadoussac and its director André Tremblay, for together they have helped make Tadoussac a world-class youth destination.

Since 1974, the youth hostel has been full almost year round. It is a crossroads of many languages and cultures that meet in a laid-back atmosphere where friendship is

the order of the day and pleasure a common goal. Seeing the young and not so young hostellers, especially sitting around a campfire with guitars, you'd almost think time had stopped in the seventies.

Also called "Maison Majorique", the youth hostel is one of the most important accommodations of its kind in the country. Reconstructed in 1994 after a fire, it now occupies a big modern house that is traditional in style, with a warm and inviting atmosphere.

Bibliography

ARMSTRONG, Joe C. W., **Samuel de Champlain**, Montréal, Les Éditions de l'Homme, 1988, 385 pages.

BOUCHARD, Russel, **Le Saguenay des fourrures (Histoire d'un monopole)**, Russel Bouchard, Chicoutimi, 1989, 269 pages.

BOUGAINVILLE, Louis-Antoine de, **Journal de Bougainville**, in RAPQ, 1923-1924, Québec, L.-A. Proulx Imprimeur, 1924, p. 310.

BUIES, Arthur, **Le Saguenay et la Vallée du lac Saint-Jean**, Imprimerie de A. Côté et Cie, Québec, 1880, pp. 81 and 82.

BULLETIN DU PARC MARIN SAGUENAY-SAINT-LAURENT, **Baleines sous observation**, Tadoussac, May 1998, p. 7.

CHAMPLAIN, Samuel de, **Oeuvres complètes**, vol. 1, Éditions du Jour, Montréal, 1971, 474 pages.

Commission de toponymie, **Noms et lieux du Québec, dictionnaire illustré**, Les publications du Québec, Québec, 1994, 925 pages.

DESBIENS, Danny, **Étude ethno-historique du hameau du Moulin-Baude**, Parc marin Saguenay–Saint-Laurent & Parc du Saguenay, Tadoussac, 1992, 63 pages.

DRAINVILLE, Gérard, "Le fjord du Saguenay: 1, Contribution à l'océanographie", **Le Naturaliste Canadien**, vol. 95, no. 4, 1968, pp. 809 to 855.

GIRARD, Camil and Normand PERRON, **Histoire du Saguenay – Lac-Saint-Jean**, Institut québécois de recherche sur la culture, Québec, 1989, 665 pages.

GIRARD, Camil and Jean-Michel TREMBLAY, **Les Saguenay–Lac-Saint-Jean en 1850**, Sagamie/Québec, Jonquière, 1988, p. 11.

L'ÉQUIPE DE RÉTABLISSEMENT DU BÉLUGA DU SAINT-LAURENT, **Plan de rétablissement du béluga du Saint-Laurent**, Pêches et Océans et Fonds mondial pour la nature, Canada, 1995, 73 pages.

LACASSE, R. P. Zach, **Une mine produisant l'or et l'argent**, Ministère de l'Agriculture du Québec, Québec, 1880, 272 pages.

LACOURSIÈRE, Jacques, **Histoire populaire du Québec, des origines à 1791**, Tome 1, Septentrion, Sillery, 1995, 480 pages.

LAFRENIÈRE, Normand, **Lightkeeping on the St. Lawrence: The End of an Era**, Dundurn Press/Parks Canada, Toronto, 1996, 125 pages.

LEMOINE, J. M., **Album du Touriste**, Sillery, 1872, 382 pages.

MICHAUD, Robert, "Les 13 baleines du Saint-Laurent", Les baleines du Saint-Laurent, supplément au magazine **Québec-Science**, GREMM, Tadoussac, June 1999, pp. 8-9.

MICHAUD, Robert, **Rencontres avec les baleines du Saint-Laurent**, Tadoussac, GREMM, 1993, 74 pages.

National Geographic Field Guide to Birds of North America, National Geographic Society, 464 pages.

PARADIS, Jean, **Histoire de la station de feux d'alignement de Pointe-Noire, P.Q.**, rapport interne, Garde côtière canadienne, Région des Laurentides, s.d.

PÊCHES ET OCÉANS CANADA, Diagnostic sur les bélugas du Saint-Laurent, **Béluga (magazine)**, Vol. 5, Numéro 1, 1994, pp. 7 and 8.

TREMBLAY, Victor, **Histoire du Saguenay depuis les origines jusqu'à 1870**, La Librairie régionale Inc., Chicoutimi, 1968, 465 pages.

TREMBLAY, Victor, **Le découvreur du Canada**, Publications de la Société historique du Saguenay, Chicoutimi, 1970, p. 60.

VILLENEUVE, Gaby, **Musée maritime Tadoussac, textes de l'exposition 1999**, Musée maritime de Tadoussac, Tadoussac, 1999, 16 pages.

VILLENEUVE, Gaby, **Les vieilles familles de Tadoussac, 1850-1950**, published by the author, Tadoussac, 1997, 136 pages.

Archival photo credits

p. 7. S. J. Hayward, **Tadoussac**, s.d., ANQ-Q P547, CPN 799-2.

p. 21. Map. Printing by Charlevoix Offset. Retouching by Julie Benoît.

p. 22. From top to bottom. **View of Tadoussac**, coll. Livernois ca. 1864, ANC, PA 138946; H. Lavoie, **Tadoussac**, 1942, ANC-Q, E6-S7-P10213; **Tadoussac circa 1867**, ANC, PA 51710.

p. 23. Centre, private coll. C. Morin; right, A. Henderson, **Anse à l'eau near Tadoussac, Mouth of Saguenay River**, coll. Sir Sandford Fleming, ANC, C74785; below, plate from the **Canadian Illustrated News**, August 26, 1971, ANC, C 50332.

p. 54. Pinsonneault et Frères, **Tadoussac**, s.d., ANQ-Q, P 547, CPN 799-3.

p. 61. Plate from **Canadian Illustrated News**, August 26, 1971, ANC, C50332;

p. 64. Above, Plate from **Canadian Illustrated News**, August 26, 1971, ANC, C50332; left, **Anse-à-l'eau, Tadoussac Landing**, s.d., coll. Livernois, ANC, PA 23841.

p. 71. Left, Valentine & Sons, **Tadoussac**, s.d., ANQ-Q, P 547, CPC 799-1; right, **Hôtel Tadoussac, circa 1880**, ANC PA 23521.

p. 73. Centre, **Hôtel Tadoussac**, ca. 1865, ANC, PA 143587; below, **Hotel staff**, 1960s, private coll. Fleurette Harvey-Maher.

p. 78. Anglican chapel, s.d., private coll. Fleurette Harvey-Maher.

p. 82. Above, L. Evans, **Le Noroît**, private coll. L. Evans; below, **A Canada Steamship Lines vessel arrives at its port of call, Tadoussac**, ANQ-Q, N 78-2-12-27.

p. 83. Above, S. J. Hayward, **Tadoussac**, s.d., ANQ-Q P547, CPN 799-2; left, menu from the St. Lawrence, 1942, private coll. Gaby Villeneuve.

p. 84. Above, **the Québec in flames, August 14, 1950**, private coll. Fleurette Harvey-Maher; below, **the Jacques-Cartier**, private coll. Rosette Deschênes.

p. 91. Porpoise hunters, private coll. Bertrand Therrien.

p. 112. Valentine & Sons, **Government Hatchery for Salmon Trout, Tadoussac, Que., Lower St. Lawrence River**, s.d., ANQ-Q, p 547, CPC 799-2.